Easter Activity Book for Pre-K

Tip:

Get extra tracing practice by creating reusable sheets!

1. Cut out the tracing pages.

2. Place individual tracing pages into sheet protectors.

3. Write on the sheets with dry erase markers.

4. Wipe marker off of sheet protector to reuse.

Hello!

I hope you have fun completing the activities in this book!

If you like this book, please ask a grown up to help you write a review on Amazon!

Your thoughtful comments and kind reviews inspire me to make more fun books for kids just like you.

Thank you,

Dawn L. Alexander

WANT THE FREE BONUS PAGES?

Email me at

authordawnlalexander@gmail.com

with the subject "Easter Activity" and we'll send your free printable BONUS Activity Pack!

Easter Activity Book for Pre-K
Copyright © 2021 Dawn L Alexander
All rights reserved. No part of this publication may be reproduced, distributed or transmitted in any form or by any means, including photocopying, recording, or other electronic or mechanical means, without prior written permission of the publisher, except in the case of brief quotations embodied in critical reviews and certain other noncommercial uses permitted by copyright law.

This Activity Book Belongs to:

_____

_____

Shapes and Colors

Color the egg with squares green.
Color the egg with circles orange.
Color the egg with triangles yellow.
Color the egg with rectangles blue.
Color the egg with stars purple.
Color the egg with hearts red.

Matching Game
Draw a line to connect each matching pair.

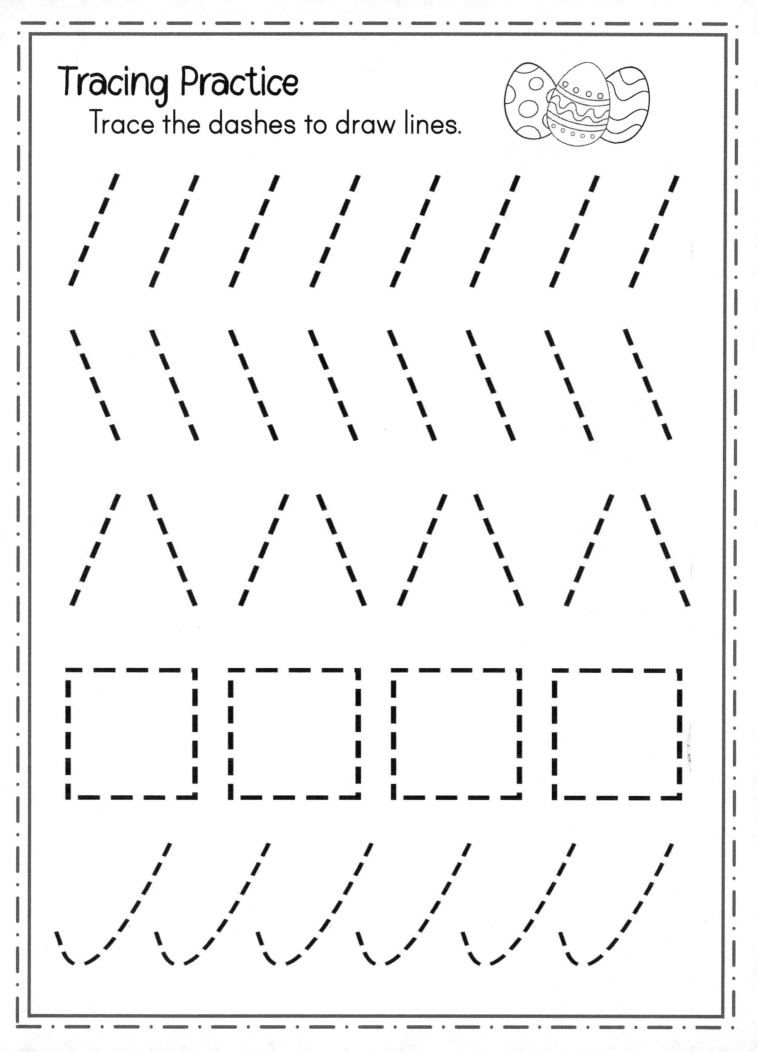

Tracing Practice

Trace and color the eggs.

Tracing Practice

Trace the dashed lines on the egg.

Tracing Practice

Trace the dotted lines.

Trace the Number

0

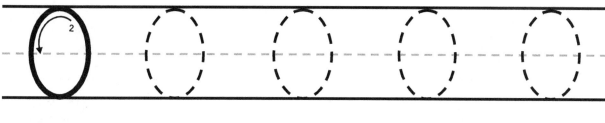

zero zero zero

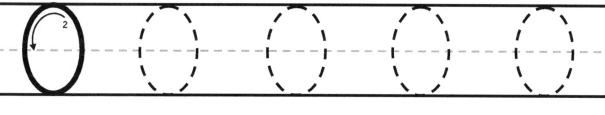

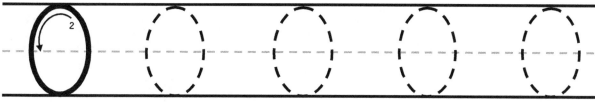

How Many Eggs Do You See?
Count 123 And Color

Trace the Number

1

one one one

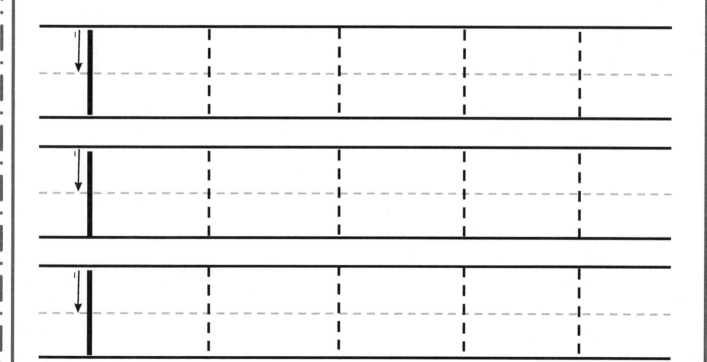

How Many Balls Do You See?
Count 123 And Color

Trace the Number

2

two two two

2 2 2 2 2 2
2 2 2 2 2 2
2 2 2 2 2 2

Trace the Number

3

three three three

3 3 3 3 3 3 3
3 3 3 3 3 3 3
3 3 3 3 3 3 3

Trace the Number

4

four four four

4 4 4 4 4 4
4 4 4 4 4 4
4 4 4 4 4 4

Trace the Number

5

five five five

Trace the Number

6

six six six

6 6 6 6 6 6
6 6 6 6 6 6
6 6 6 6 6 6

Trace the Number

7

seven seven seven

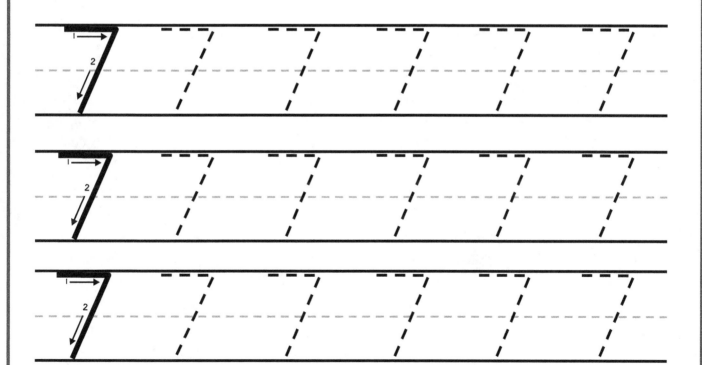

Trace the Number

8

eight eight eight

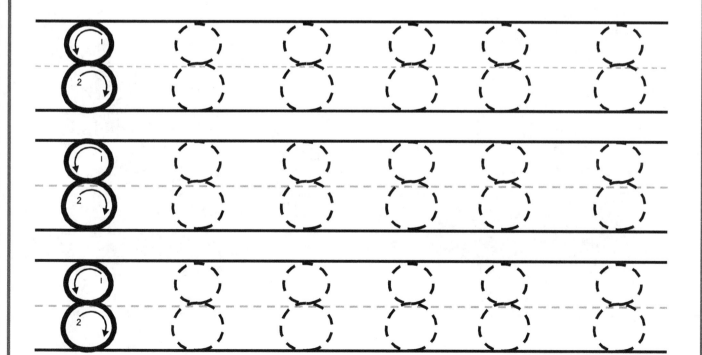

How Many Buttons Do You See?
Count 123 And Color

Trace the Number

9

nine nine nine

9 9 9 9 9 9

9 9 9 9 9 9

9 9 9 9 9 9

Trace the Number

10

ten ten ten

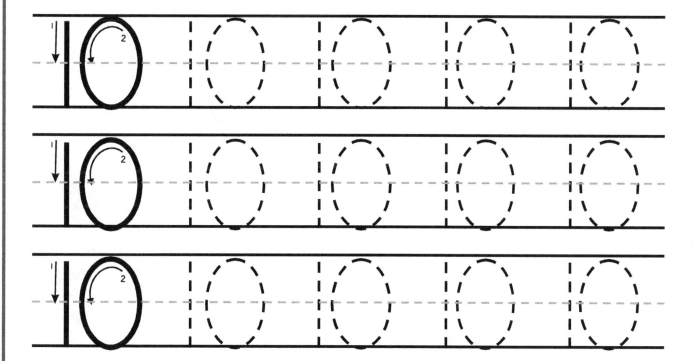

Word Search

Find the words in the letter grid., then circle them.

G	C	D	C	G	C	E	T	C	O
Y	F	E	C	U	V	G	C	H	U
J	K	C	A	T	B	G	H	O	G
B	H	O	R	H	O	S	U	C	B
U	E	R	R	O	N	J	R	O	C
N	E	A	O	P	N	X	C	L	C
N	C	T	T	K	E	H	H	A	A
Y	T	E	I	Y	T	C	T	T	N
Z	T	E	A	S	T	E	R	E	D
D	Y	E	P	L	I	L	Y	V	Y

Easter   candy   bonnet
hop   lily   church
bunny   chocolate   dye
carrot   eggs   decorate

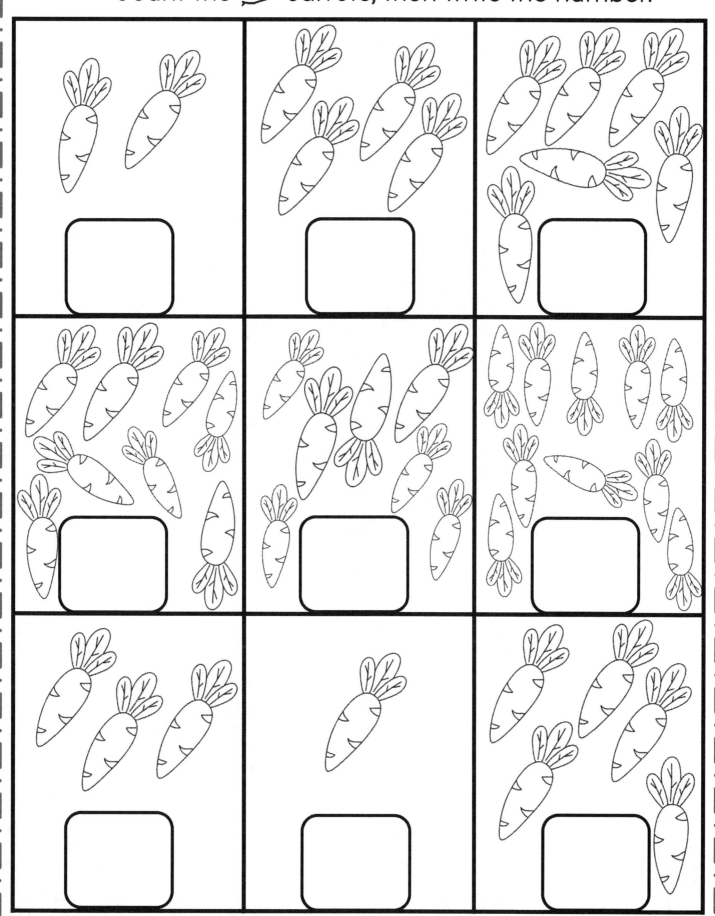

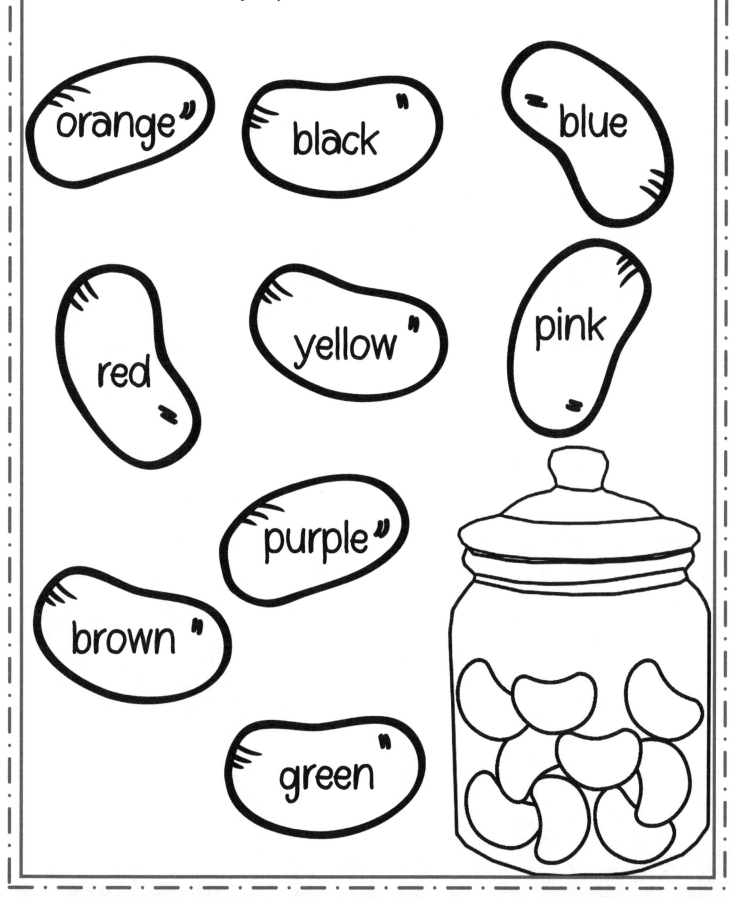

Word Search

Find the words in the letter grid., then circle them.

H	U	N	T	H	L	A	M	B	V
J	L	P	A	R	A	D	E	G	W
E	C	M	D	W	C	H	I	C	K
L	A	Y	Y	S	P	R	I	N	G
L	J	N	U	J	G	S	V	F	R
Y	J	N	L	Z	J	P	S	A	A
B	A	S	K	E	T	O	T	I	S
E	F	L	O	W	E	R	S	T	S
A	F	F	A	M	I	L	Y	H	E
N	S	U	N	D	A	Y	J	Y	Z

basket   hunt   flowers

lamb   chick   jelly bean

grass   family   faith

spring   Sunday   parade

Count and Color
Color the correct number of flowers.

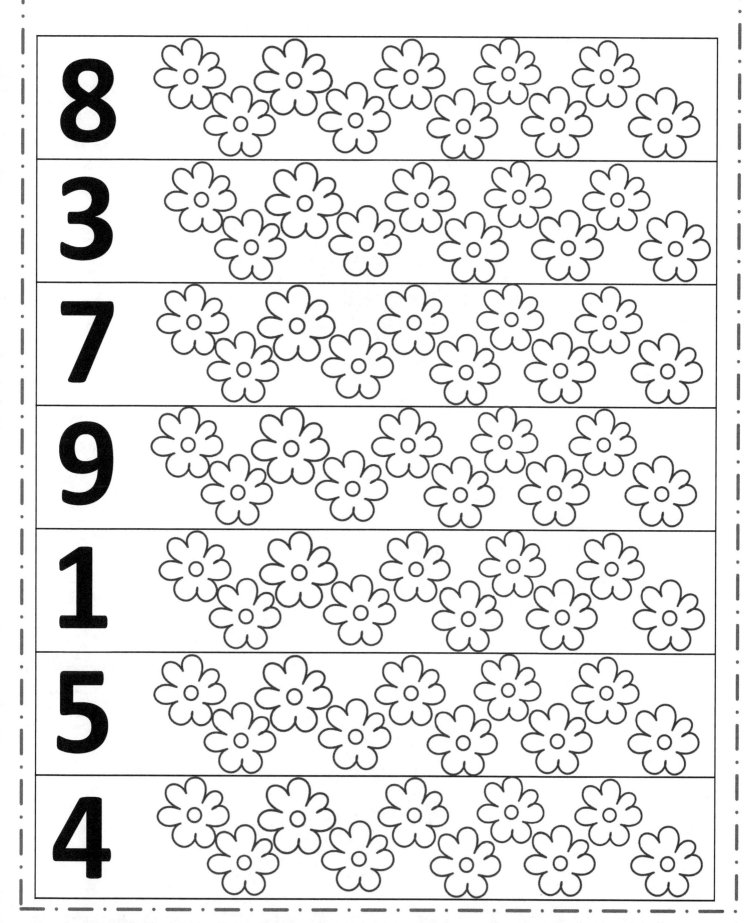

Letter Matching

Draw lines to connect each uppercase letter to its lowercase match.

Count and Color
Color the correct number of jelly beans.

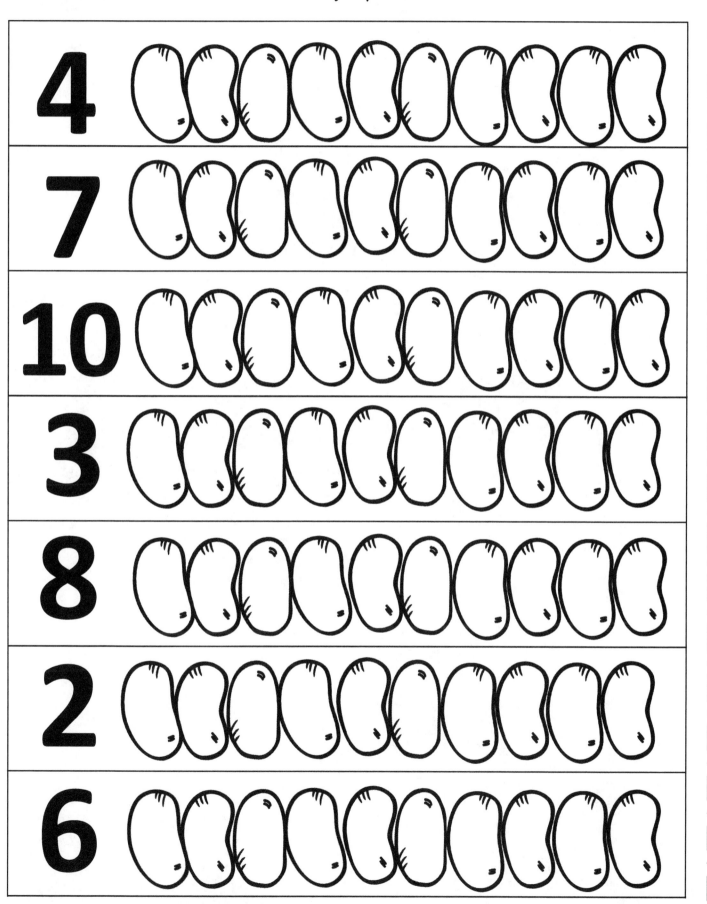

Maze

Help the bunny find his basket.

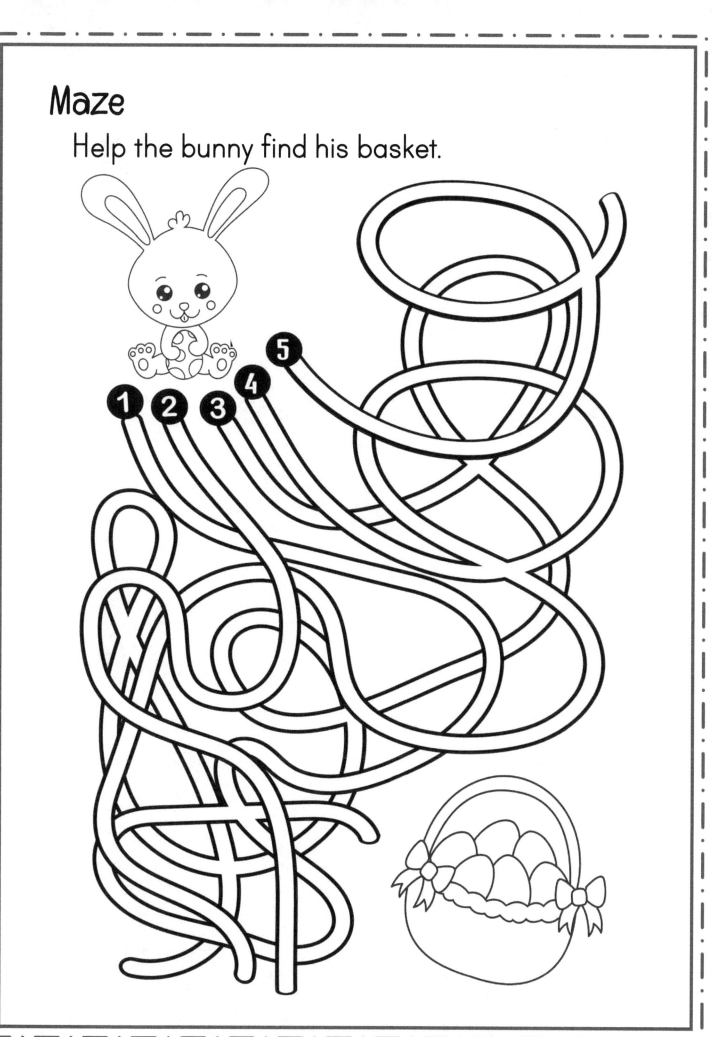

Color by Number

Use the code to color the picture.

- 1 = blue
- 2 = pink
- 3 = yellow
- 4 = purple
- 5 = brown
- 6 = orange
- 7 = green
- 8 = white
- 9 = black

Ten Frames

Color the ten frames to match the number on the carrot.

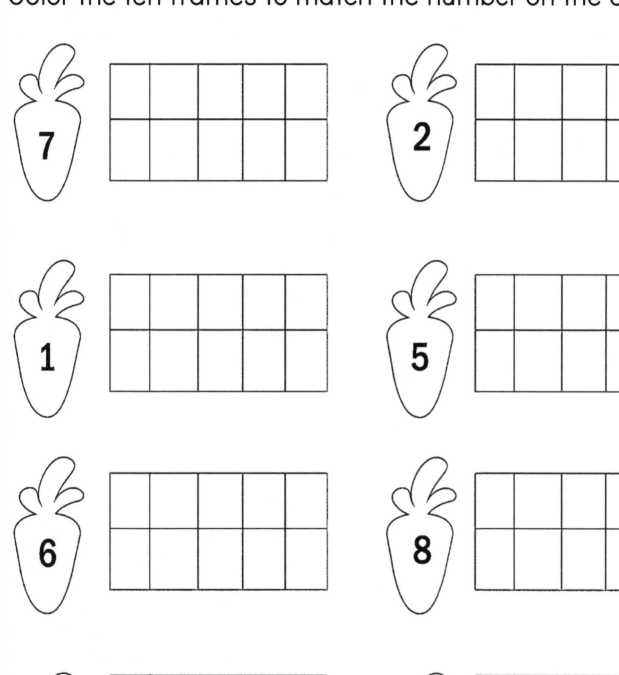

Ten Frames

Color the ten frames to match the number on the rabbit.

Butterfly Symmetry

Draw circles to make the butterfly wings match.

How Many Jelly Beans?

Count the jelly beans and circle the correct number.

I Spy

Circle five pictures that start with the letter B.

Spot the Differences
Circle the five things that are different in the picture below, then color the picture.

Letter Tracing

Trace the upper case letter of the alphabet on each egg.

Letter Tracing

Trace the lower case letter of the alphabet on each egg.

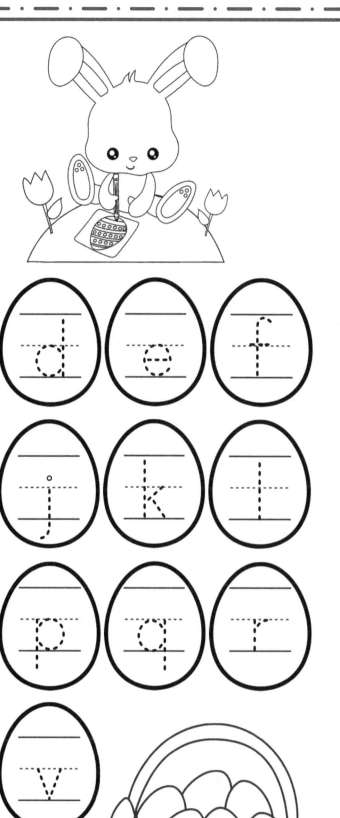

a b c d e f
g h i j k l
m n o p q r
s t u v
w x y z

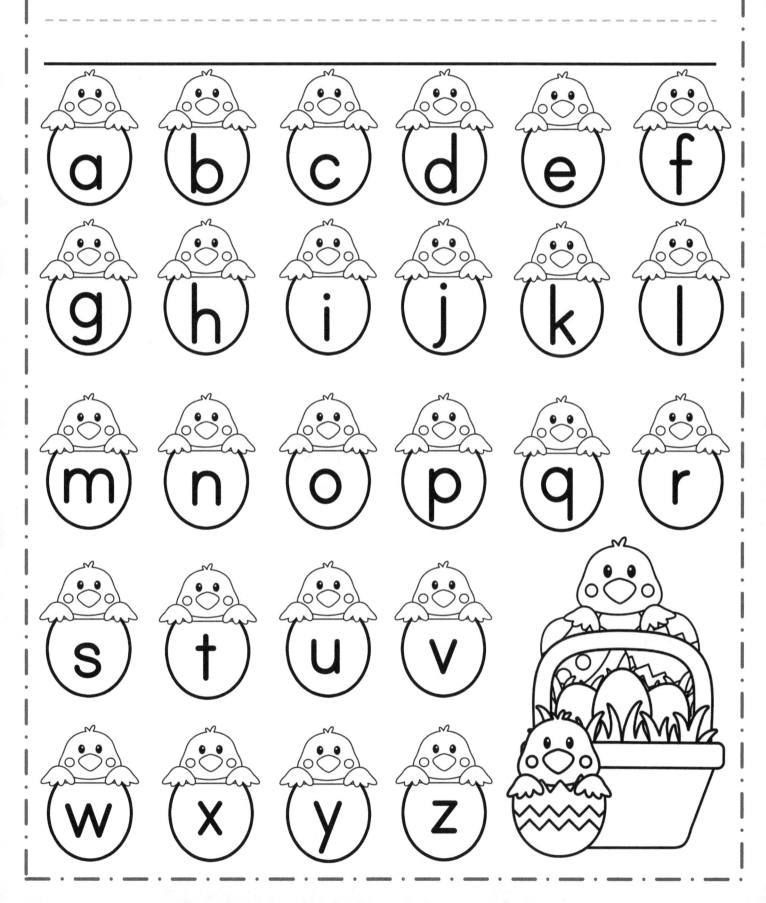

Word Search

Find the words in the letter grid, then circle them.

L	W	N	C	W	U	R	E	D	C
E	G	G	W	H	I	T	E	P	Q
O	N	R	C	O	L	O	R	U	X
R	J	E	U	K	P	B	Y	R	W
A	B	E	B	P	I	L	Y	P	O
N	L	N	R	V	N	U	E	L	T
G	A	P	O	U	K	E	L	E	W
R	C	G	W	Y	X	P	L	J	K
B	K	T	N	J	E	P	O	R	R
C	A	R	M	Z	J	S	W	Y	K

egg   color   pink
red   green   white
yellow   purple   blue
orange   black   brown

I Spy   How many of each can you find in the box?

How many all together? _____

Color by Letters

Use the code to color the picture.

S = blue   A = purple   Y = green
E = pink   R = brown   O = gray
T = yellow H = orange   P = red

CPSIA information can be obtained
at www.ICGtesting.com
Printed in the USA
LVHW060950140323
741578LV00016B/119

9 798706 975814